SHAPING THE WORLD

CHOSEN BY
LIZ BROWNLEE

40 HISTORICAL HEROES IN VERSE

Other poetry titles available from Macmillan Children's Books

Reaching the Stars

Poems about Extraordinary Women and Girls

Jan Dean, Liz Brownlee and Michaela Morgan

The Same Inside

Poems about Empathy and Friendship

Liz Brownlee, Matt Goodfellow and Roger Stevens

Be the Change

Poems to Help You Save the World

Liz Brownlee, Matt Goodfellow and Roger Stevens

SHAPING THE WORLD

CHOSEN BY
LIZ BROWNLEE

40 HISTORICAL HEROES IN VERSE

MACMILLAN
CHILDREN'S BOOKS

First published 2021 by Macmillan Children's Books
an imprint of Pan Macmillan
The Smithson, 6 Briset Street, London EC1M 5NR
EU representative: Macmillan Publishers Ireland Limited,
Mallard Lodge, Lansdowne Village, Dublin 4
Associated companies throughout the world
www.panmacmillan.com

ISBN 978-1-5290-3686-2

1 3 5 7 9 8 6 4 2

A CIP catalogue record for this book is available from the British Library.

Printed and bound by CPI Group (UK) Ltd, Croydon CR0 4YY
Designed by The Dimpse

FSC www.fsc.org MIX Paper from responsible sources FSC® C116313

CONTENTS

For Emmelie and Jake,
helping to shape a greener future.

Greta Thunberg, born 2003, Inspiring Action Against Climate Crisis

In 2018, the first of the school climate strikes were started by schoolgirl Greta Thunberg. Thunberg was born in Stockholm, Sweden.

FAMOUS FOR: When she read information about the climate crisis, Thunberg became overwhelmed. She was baffled as to why the world's governments were not taking action. Aged fifteen, she won a writing competition, asking why politicians lie about climate crisis facts.

Every Friday, she started to school strike for climate outside the Swedish parliament. Her posts about it on Instagram and Twitter went viral. Thunberg inspired millions of children in over a hundred countries to strike for their future on the planet. They asked their own governments to take action, and tell the truth about the climate crisis.

FASCINATING FACTS: Greta Thunberg has Asperger's Syndrome and calls it her superpower. The climate crisis groups she has made speeches to include the UN Climate Change Conference and the European parliament. She won Amnesty International's Ambassador of Conscience Award in 2019 and was nominated for a Nobel Peace Prize in 2019 and 2021.

QUOTES: 'Why should I be studying for a future that soon may be no more, when no one is doing anything to save that future?'

'What is the point of learning facts when the most important facts clearly mean nothing to our society?'

Start at the top side of her head, read two lines, then read the three lines on the left side of her hair, up through her fringe, then the right side of her hair.

Truth

Liz Brownlee

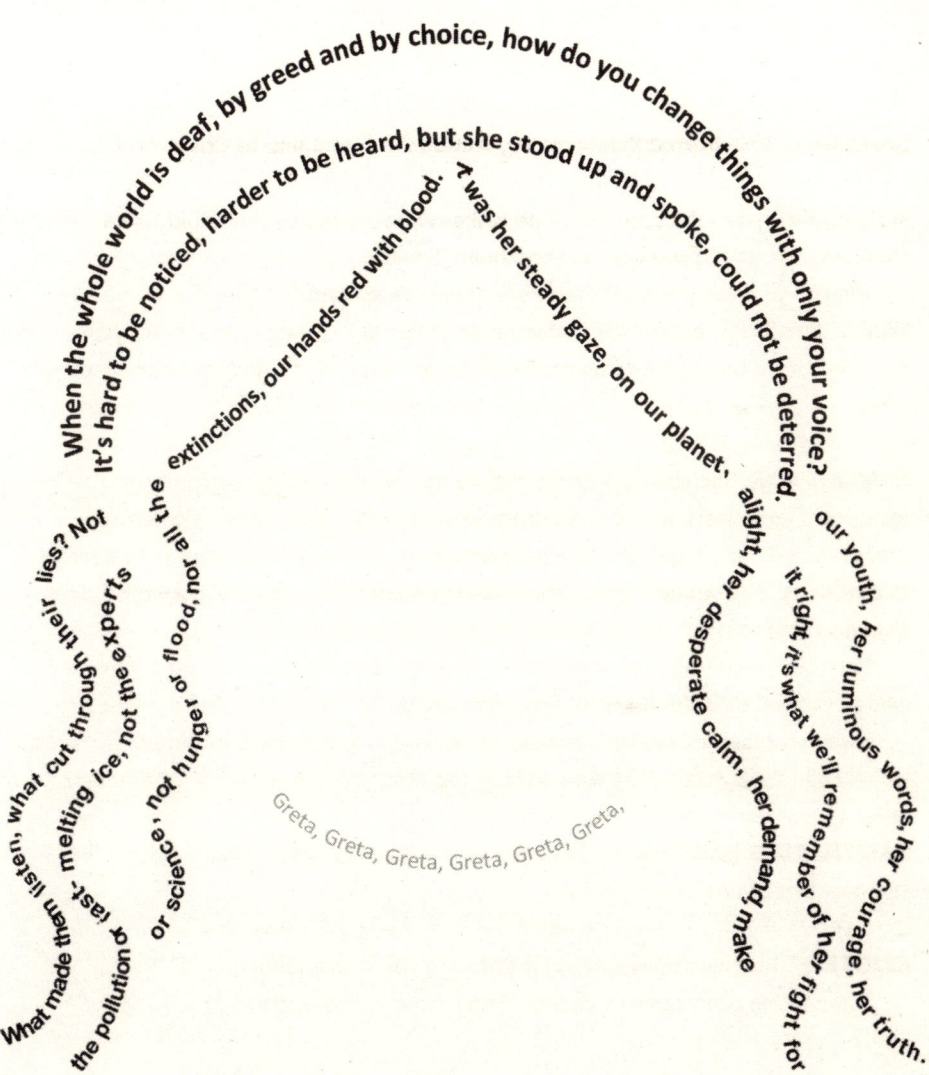

When the whole world is deaf, by greed and by choice, how do you change things with only your voice?
It's hard to be noticed, harder to be heard, but she stood up and spoke, could not be deterred.
What made them listen, what cut through their lies? Not
the pollution or last-, melting ice, not the experts
or science, not hunger or flood, nor all the
extinctions, our hands red with blood.
It was her steady gaze, on our planet,
alight, her desperate calm, her demand, make
it right, it's what we'll remember of her fight for
our youth, her luminous words, her courage, her truth.

Greta, Greta, Greta, Greta, Greta, Greta,

Socrates, c. 470–399 BC, Philosopher, Devised a System to Seek the Truth

About 2,490 years ago, the Greek philosopher Socrates was born in Alopeke, Greece. He is considered to be one of the founders of Western philosophy. Philosophy is the exploration of ideas using thinking skills. It asks questions like: Why are we here? What is truth? How are we connected to the universe? He wrote nothing down but his teachings have been passed on by his students, including another great philosopher, Plato.

FAMOUS FOR: Socrates' wisdom and problem solving methods are still used today. He is most famous for the Socratic method of enquiry. This is used to examine morals such as good and justice. To solve a problem, it is broken down into a series of questions. The answers gradually reveal the solution a person is looking for. The Socratic method is still used in American legal education!

Socrates' beliefs were his downfall in the end. He questioned his government, and was sentenced to death by drinking poison hemlock.

Socrates accepted his fate because he had been found guilty of something he had done. Even though he felt he was right, it was against the law.

FASCINATING FACT: Plato reported that Socrates drank the poison without the slightest hint of hesitation.

QUOTES: 'The only true wisdom is in knowing you know nothing.'

'I am not an Athenian or a Greek, but a citizen of the world.'

Start at the top and read down the outside of the question mark, then go to the top inside of the question mark, then read the circle.

The Socratic Method

Jane Clarke

What is art? What is courage? What is love? What is truth? What do you know? How do you know it? Debate with one another.

Thought is critical. Think, think, think. Question assumptions, evidence, attitudes, viewpoints, concepts, knowledge.

Question the question.

Frances Glessner Lee, 1878–1962, First Forensic Pathologist, Helped Solve Murders

In 1945, Frances Glessner Lee became the first person to teach Crime Scene Detection. She was born into a rich family in Illinois, the United States, and taught at home. Glessner Lee was not allowed to go to university. Her father felt that 'a lady didn't go to school'. However, the crafts she learned from her mother and aunts proved useful later in life.

FAMOUS FOR: After inheriting her family's fortune, Glessner Lee was able to follow her interest in forensic pathology. Forensic pathologists find out how and why someone has died. She studied how detectives examine and draw conclusions from clues.

From 1945, Glessner Lee started giving talks to the police to train them in the art and science of crime scene investigation. She showed the students detailed models she had made of actual crime scenes. These were called dioramas and each one took about six months to build. They had working windows, doors and lights, as well as blood-splattered floors and figures to represent the murder victims. Glessner Lee called her dioramas the 'Nutshell Studies of Unexplained Death'.

FASCINATING FACTS: Glessner Lee was fascinated by the stories of Sherlock Holmes, who solved crimes by attention to detail. Eighteen of the original twenty dioramas she made are *still* used for training purposes by Harvard Associates in Police Science.

QUOTE: 'As the investigator, you must bear in mind that there is a two-fold responsibility – to clear the innocent as well as expose the guilty. Seek only the facts – find the truth in a nutshell.'

Start at the words 'Look inside' and read left to right all the way to the bottom, finishing off at the knife.

In a Nutshell

Cheryl Moskowitz

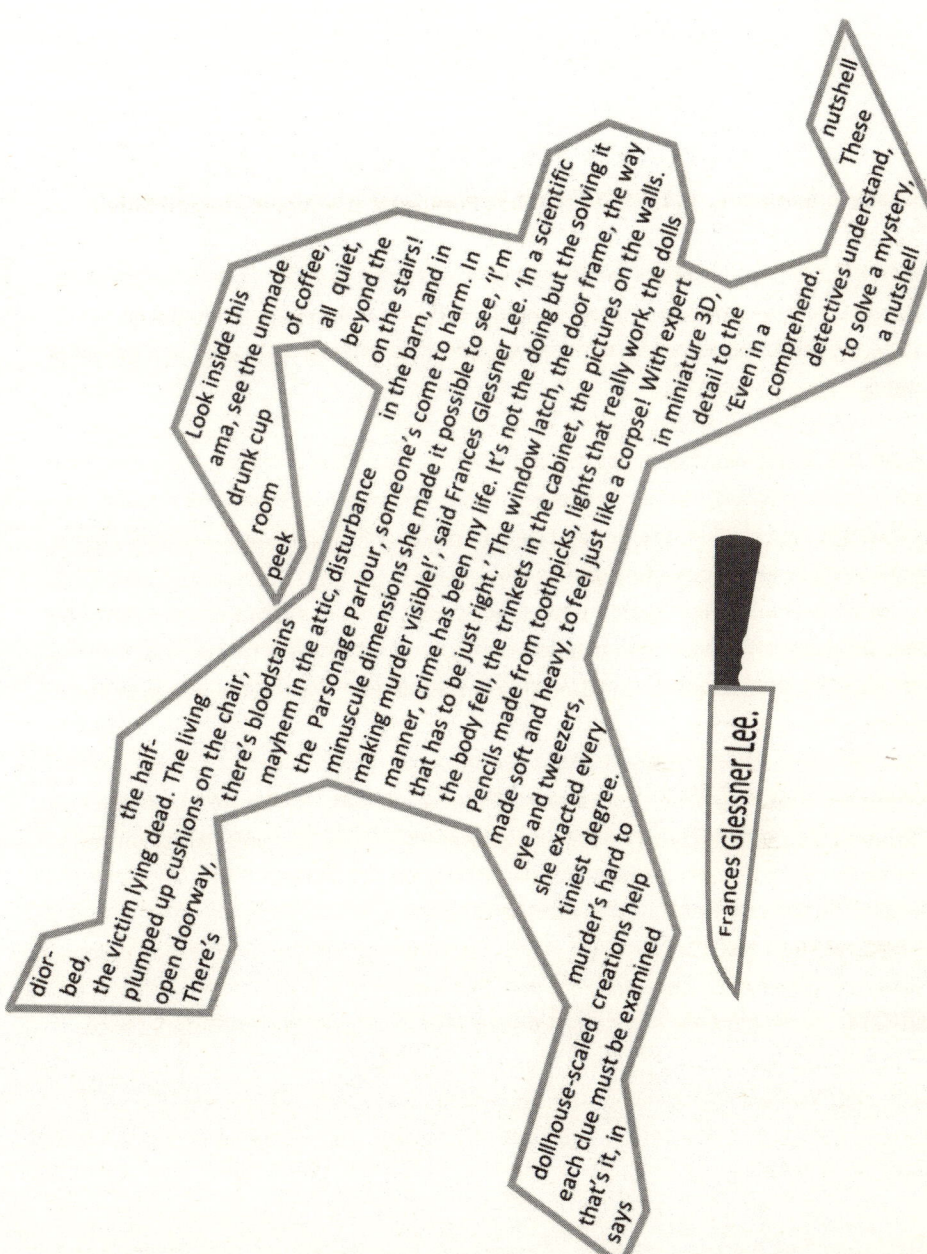

Look inside this dior-
ama, see the unmade bed,
the half-drunk cup of coffee,
the victim lying dead. The living room all quiet,
plumped up cushions on the chair,
peek beyond the open doorway,
there's bloodstains on the stairs!
There's mayhem in the attic, disturbance in the barn, and in
the Parsonage Parlour, someone's come to harm. In
minuscule dimensions she made it possible to see, 'I'm
making murder visible!', said Frances Glessner Lee. 'In a scientific
manner, crime has been my life. It's not the doing but the solving it
that has to be just right.' The window latch, the door frame, the way
the body fell, the trinkets in the cabinet, the pictures on the walls.
Pencils made from toothpicks, lights that really work, the dolls
made soft and heavy, to feel just like a corpse! With expert
eye and tweezers, in miniature 3D,
she exacted every detail to the
tiniest degree. 'Even in a nutshell
murder's hard to comprehend. These
dollhouse-scaled creations help detectives understand,
each clue must be examined to solve a mystery,
that's it, in a nutshell
says Frances Glessner Lee.

Elizabeth Blackwell, 1821–1910, First Female Doctor in the United States

In 1849, Elizabeth Blackwell made history by becoming the first female doctor in the United States. She was born to a rich family in Bristol, England, and was taught at home, by private teachers. When she was eleven, her family emigrated to the United States.

FAMOUS FOR: After her family lost their fortune, Blackwell and her sisters opened a school to earn money. When one of her friends became ill, she said she wouldn't have suffered so much, if her doctor had been a woman. This experience made Blackwell became more and more interested in medicine.

Blackwell had to fight extreme prejudice to get her training as a doctor. It was not seen as a suitable job for a woman. Eventually she found a university willing to admit her. In 1847, she became the first woman to attend medical school in the United States.

FASCINATING FACTS: All the male students had to agree to Blackwell being admitted for training. They all said yes – and at the end of the course she came top of her class. When she was presented with her degree, the dean of the university bowed to her. She went on to set up the first training school for female doctors in the United Kingdom.

QUOTE: 'None of us can know what we are capable of until we are tested.'

Start at the first earpiece, read the left-hand arm top and bottom, middle two lines top and bottom, and right-hand arm top and bottom. Then read the tubing right side then left side, the middle and then the outside of the circle.

Elizabeth Blackwell

Penny Kent

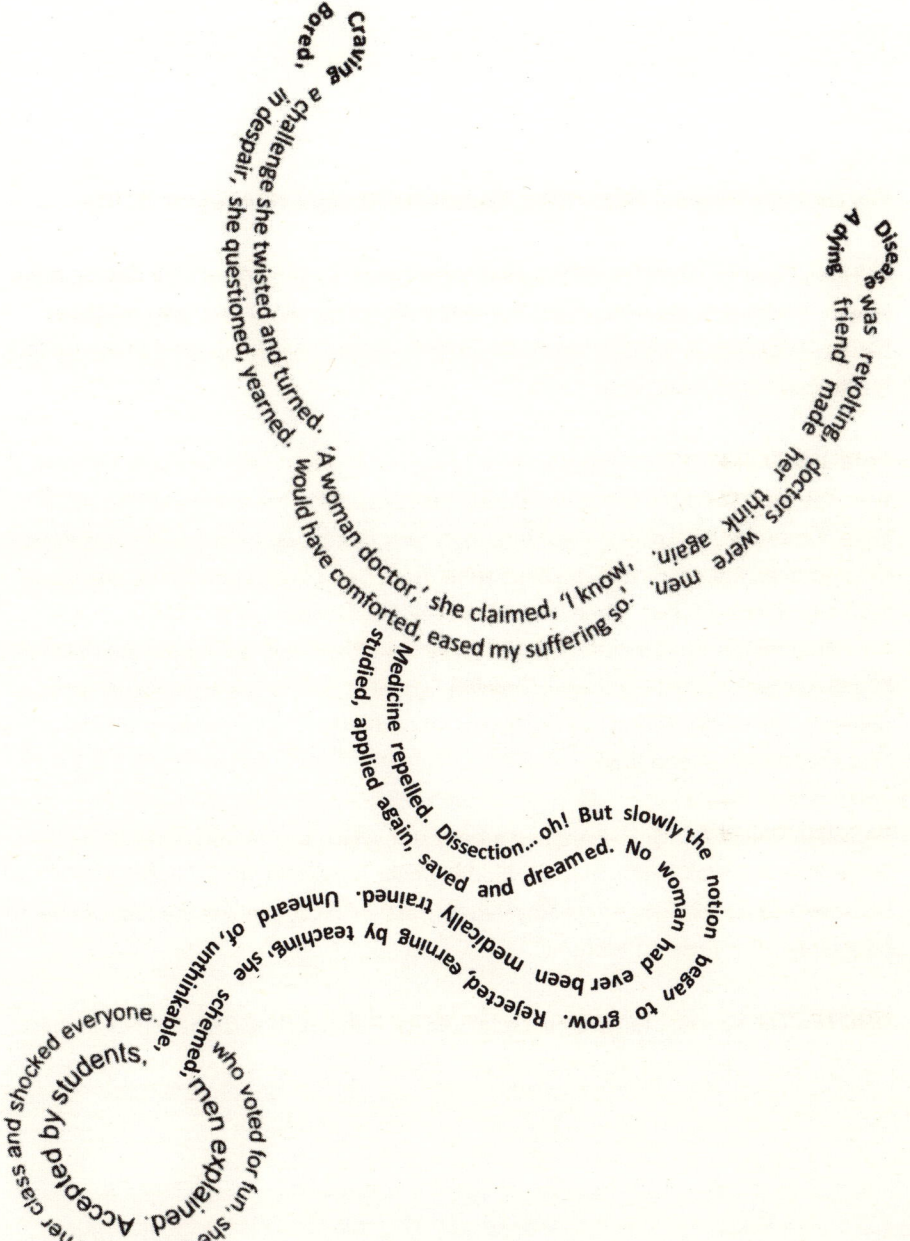

Craving a challenge she twisted and turned.
Bored, in despair, she questioned, yearned.
Disease was revolting, doctors were men.
A dying friend made her think again.
'A woman doctor,' she claimed, 'I know,
would have comforted, eased my suffering so.'
Medicine repelled. Dissection…oh!
But slowly the notion began to grow.
Rejected, earning by teaching, she schemed,
studied, applied again, saved and dreamed.
No woman had ever been medically trained.
Unheard of, unthinkable, men explained.
Accepted by students, who voted for fun,
she came top of her class and shocked everyone.

Florence Nightingale, 1820–1910, Founder of Modern Nursing

In 1860, Florence Nightingale founded her modern nursing school. She was born to wealthy British parents in Italy, and her father taught her as a child. When she was sixteen, Nightingale felt God was calling her to devote her life to caring. She decided He wanted her to be a nurse.

FAMOUS FOR: In 1854, Nightingale heard about soldiers suffering in the Crimean War. She went to help them at the British base hospital in the Crimea taking thirty-eight nurses she had trained. Realising that many deaths were from lack of cleanliness, she improved the conditions. Soldiers were given clean sheets and bandages, good food and drinking water. She even had the sewers cleaned.

A Nightingale Fund was set up in recognition of her work during the war. With this money she set up the Nightingale Training School at St Thomas' Hospital in London, England. The methods used by her nurses helped reduce the number of deaths in the First and Second World Wars.

FASCINATING FACTS: She rescued a baby owl, which she named Athena. Sometimes she took it round wards, hidden in her pocket. In 1883, Nightingale became the first recipient of the Royal Red Cross. In 1907, she was the first woman to be awarded the Order of Merit.

QUOTE: 'The very first requirement in a hospital is that it should do the sick no harm.'

Start from the top, 'My mistress has a gentle face', left to right all the way down.

Florence Nightingale and Athena

Sue Hardy-Dawson

My mistress has a
gentle face
Her hands are clean and cool
A lamp for a
nightingale, a pocket
for an owl. They shook
their heads at fresh air, at rats
beneath the beds. *Cleanliness!*
They mocked her, as they carried
out their dead. My mistress took
a fine, stiff brush, scrubbed her
fingers raw. She opened every
window, wrapped her patients
clean and warm. She shook
her head at gangrene, the
stench of rotten flesh,
the
She boiled up all
linen and made sure the sick were fed. My mistress has a gentle face,
she has an angel's soul. A lamp for a nightingale, a pocket for an owl.

Anne Frank, 1929–1945, Holocaust Victim, Wrote *The Diary of a Young Girl*

In 1945, Anne Frank died, aged just fifteen. Annelies Marie Frank was born into a Jewish family in Frankfurt, Germany. In 1934, her family emigrated to Amsterdam in the Netherlands.

FAMOUS FOR: The German army invaded the Netherlands a year after the Second World War began. The Nazis immediately discriminated against Jewish people. In 1942, they made all Jewish people wear a yellow badge with a six-pointed star on, the Star of David. It had the Dutch word 'Jood' on it, meaning 'Jew'. The Jewish people became scared of what would happen to them.

Anne Frank's family hid for two years in secret rooms in her father's workplace. She wrote her famous diary about her life there. In 1944, the Secret Annex was discovered and the family were arrested and sent to concentration camps. Frank died in 1945, just two months before the end of the war.

FASCINATING FACT: Anne Frank was given her diary for her thirteenth birthday. It was actually an autograph book. After filling it, she went on to use two notebooks and loose paper. Anne's diary has been translated into seventy languages with over thirty million copies sold. Her message of hope in the face of adversity has inspired people around the world.

QUOTES: 'I believe in the sun, even when it rains.'

'How wonderful it is that no one has to wait, but can start right now to gradually change the world!'

Start at 'An ordinary child' and read round the first triangle, then from 'A personal diary' round the second triangle.

Anne Frank

John Dougherty

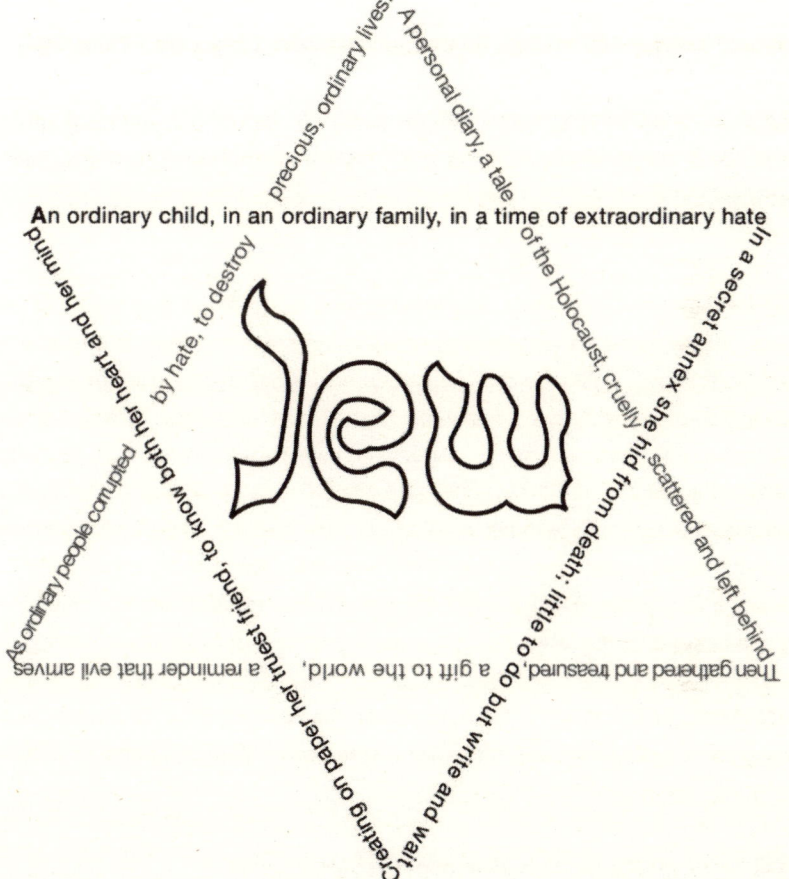

An ordinary child, in an ordinary family, in a time of extraordinary hate
In a secret annex she hid from death; little to do but write and wait
Creating on paper her truest friend, to know both her heart and her mind
A personal diary, a tale of the Holocaust, cruelly scattered and left behind
Then gathered and treasured, a gift to the world, a reminder that evil arrives
As ordinary people corrupted by hate, to destroy precious, ordinary lives.

Jew

Alexander Fleming, 1881–1955, Microbiologist Who Discovered Penicillin

In 1928, Alexander Fleming discovered penicillin. He was born in Darvel, Scotland. When he was older he started working in a shipping office, but didn't enjoy it. He then changed track and trained for a medical degree, and became interested in studying bacteria.

FAMOUS FOR: In 1927, Fleming was investigating a bacterium that often caused infection. Unfortunately (or fortunately!) he wasn't the most hygienic scientist. When he went on holiday in 1928, he didn't clean up his petri dishes. These were glass dishes used to grow bacteria on a jelly-like food. When he returned, he discovered fungus in one of the dishes. The 'juice' from the fungus had created a bacteria-free circle around itself.

Fleming experimented with his 'mould juice'. He found it could kill lots of deadly bacteria strains; he called it penicillin. Other scientists later developed penicillin to produce it as a drug. This first antibiotic cured many soldiers' wound infections during the Second World War.

FASCINATING FACT: In 1945, Fleming shared the Nobel Prize in Medicine for his part in penicillin's development. It has since saved more than two hundred million lives.

QUOTE: 'One sometimes finds what one is not looking for.'

Start at 'What' and read downwards, then read downwards from 'Get', then upwards from 'my'.

Fleming's Petri Dish

Laura Mucha

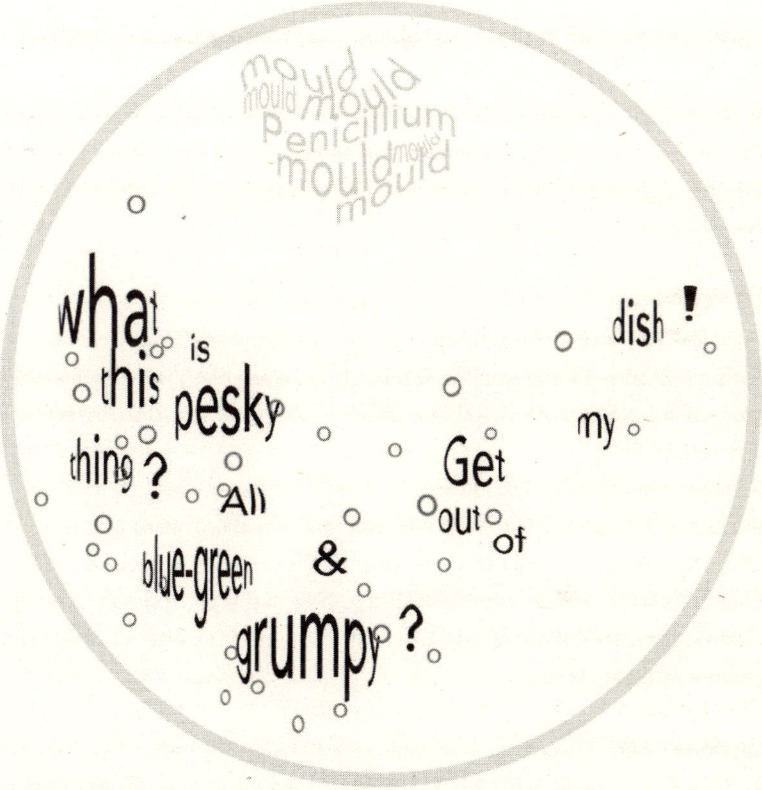
mould
mould
mould mould
Penicillium
mould mould
mould
what is this pesky thing?
All blue-green & grumpy?
Get out of my dish!

Marie Curie, 1867–1934, Discovered Radium and Helped Develop X-Rays

In 1898, Marie Curie discovered radium. Maria Sklodowska was born in Warsaw, Poland. It was her dream to be a scientist, but she could not go to any of Poland's universities because they did not admit women. She saved money to go to the Sorbonne University in Paris, France.

FAMOUS FOR: Marie Curie married Pierre Curie, another scientist, who helped her in her work. She was investigating uranium, and realised its radioactivity was coming from its atoms. Atoms are too small to see but build everything in the universe. Using her famous wash bottle (which this shape poem shows), she also discovered other radioactive materials.

Curie helped develop X-rays. During the First World War she took an X-ray machine in a car to battlefields to help sick soldiers. Her discoveries also led to radiotherapy for cancer treatments. Curie was the first woman to receive a Nobel Prize, and the first person to receive two Nobel Prizes. She is the only person to receive one in more than one science (Physics and Chemistry). She led the way for other women interested in a science career.

FASCINATING FACT: The dangers of radioactivity were not known by Curie, who carried radioactive material in the pocket of her lab coat. Her papers and even her cookery book are still too radioactive to handle.

QUOTE: 'I am among those who think that science has great beauty.'

Start at 'They' on the left of the bottle, up the left straw, then right straw, down the right of the bottle, then the lines in the bottle liquid.

Marie Curie

Kate Wakeling

They say a person's discoveries become a part of them. They say a person's discoveries have always been within them. Well those things she found, radium, polonium, if you look them up you'll find they are a thing at first to

fear. They simply cannot match this woman who
was so true and kind. But look again and see how
each beats with the same fierce heart. Discover they
are rare and strong. They are fierce. They glow with a
force that lights the air. They bring their quick beams
to bear upon the darkness that surrounds. They will
not be removed. They brim with a mighty power.
They took their time to surface to the light and
then they shone and shone and shone.

Rosalind Franklin, 1920–1958, Proved the Structure of DNA

In 1952, Rosalind Franklin took the photo that showed the structure of DNA. She was born into a wealthy family in London, England, and decided she wanted to be a scientist aged fifteen. She studied chemistry at Cambridge University.

FAMOUS FOR: In her second job, Franklin worked in Paris with crystallographer Jacques Mering. He taught her a way of taking photos of very tiny, delicate structures. Crystals are used in this process to see things usually hidden from sight.

Franklin went on to study DNA at King's College London. DNA is in every cell in the body. It acts like a computer program to tell cells what to do. Franklin took a crystallographic photo of it, which became known as Photo 51. It showed the structure of DNA. There was still prejudice against women in university jobs. Her colleague, Maurice Wilkins, secretly showed her photo to scientists Watson and Crick. They realised what it showed and published the image without mentioning that Rosalind Franklin took it.

FASCINATING FACT: Sadly Franklin died of cancer aged thirty-seven. Watson, Crick and Wilkins went on to share a Nobel Prize for their work on DNA in 1962. Franklin's work was crucial to theirs.

QUOTE: 'Science and everyday life cannot and should not be separated.'

Start at 'She' and read down the bold DNA strand of words, then from the top down the other strand of words.

Rosalind Franklin

Isabel Miles

She They
shone used
her her
data **x-rays**
for **on the**
their **very**
model **stuff**
of life of
and our
where DNA
darkness and
thanks **had**
to **been**
her **she**
they **shed**
clear got it
light right

Mary Anning, 1799–1847, Discovered Dinosaur Bones in Fossil Rocks

In 1823, Mary Anning found the first complete fossil of a plesiosaur, a large marine reptile of the Mesozoic era. She was born in the fossil-rich coastal town of Lyme Regis, England. Her family hunted for fossils in the cliffs near their home and sold them to make a living. She only went to school when she was very young. However, she read, investigated, and dissected fossilised creatures to educate herself further.

FAMOUS FOR: Anning went fossil hunting every day. She used a pointed hammer tool to break open the rocks, and expose the fossils hidden inside. Her discoveries amazed the world. Her finds changed scientific thinking about early life on Earth.

At this time, women were not allowed to vote or hold an important position. Anning wasn't allowed to join the Geological Society of London. She was admired and consulted by many of the geology experts of her time. Scientists often wrote papers about her findings, but upset her by not mentioning her name.

FASCINATING FACTS: It is thought that the tongue-twister 'She sells sea shells on the sea shore' is written about her. In 2010 the Royal Society included her in the list of the ten women who have most influenced science.

QUOTE: 'The world has used me so unkindly, I fear it has made me suspicious of everyone.'

Read left to right down the stone fossil.

Book of Stone

Mandy Coe

I'm buried deep in time but sense her walking by. *I'm here alone,* I sigh,
come find my bones. She explores the cliffs and beaches - wicker basket
on her arm. Sixty million years, I have waited, with no light, no touch,
no sound. *Come find me, come find me and take me home.*
As flat as a page in a book, I live, with no sun, no rain, no moon.
Come tell my tale, come read my story from
this book of stone. I am the treasure
she searches for: my footprints,
my teeth and my horn.
I know she is near, in the mist of dawn
and in the setting of the sun. Today, she
pauses to watch the sea. Will she hear my
whispers, quieter than the salty wind, quieter than
the waves? *Come closer, dig deeper and you will*
find me. Then, with a very gentle hand, Mary brushes the sand...

Dame Jane Goodall, born 1934, Proved Chimps Use Tools

In 1960, Jane Goodall discovered that chimpanzees make and use tools. Valerie Jane Morris-Goodall was born in London, England. As a baby she was given a stuffed chimpanzee by her father. Her love for the toy sparked her interest in animals.

FAMOUS FOR: Jane Goodall was employed by scientist Louis Leakey to study chimpanzees in Gombe Stream National Park, Africa. Until this time, scientists thought only humans used tools. Goodall watched chimpanzees using blades of grass to stick into termite mounds. They were using these tools to gather the insects to eat. In response to her findings, Leakey wrote: 'Now we must redefine tool, redefine man, or accept chimpanzees as humans.'

In 1977, she established the Jane Goodall Institute, which supports humane research into chimpanzees at the Gombe-based world-class research centre. She leads efforts to help protect chimpanzees and their habitats. In 2003, she was made a Dame of the British Empire.

FASCINATING FACT: As a child, Goodall once sat in the henhouse to wait for a hen to lay an egg. It took five hours and when she came out she found her family had reported her missing to the police.

QUOTE: 'Let us develop respect for all living things. Let us try to replace violence and intolerance with understanding and compassion. And love.'

Start from 'We' down the front of the face to 'about', the middle of the face, the back, then left to right down the body to the legs.

We did not know
the Cloud
a Bout

people… Hairless skin; moon-pale,
with soft-shoed feet.
But along came one, who, still
and gentle, watched us pick a
switch and strip its leaves, listened,
when we spoke. Or so it seemed.
Our pale moon cousin, learning
words of green. Earth sounds, the
songs of water and of tree. In her, we
saw oursel- ves, but differently.
We, who had thought them
careless and cruel, looked in her
eyes and saw no blood lust and then
we wondered, can it be true
Some are as clever,
As as us?
Sentient

Archytas, c. 410–347 BC, Invented the First Mechanical Machine

About 2420 years ago, Archytas was born in Tarentum, 'Greater Greece'. This was the name Romans gave to the southern coast in Italy. His exact birth and death dates are not known.

FAMOUS FOR: Archytas developed maths to solve mechanical problems. This is known from surviving parts of his writing, and others' accounts. Because it was so long ago, only small scraps of writing and information remain.

It was reported that Archytas designed and built a mechanical flying machine, shaped like a pigeon. It flew for about two hundred metres on its own and probably used steam. Mechanical engineering using geometry is an important tool needed for building robots. Archytas could be said to be the first person to have built a moving, mechanical robot!

FASCINATING FACTS: Archytas was a well-known general in his time. The crater Archytas on the Moon is named after him.

QUOTE: 'That tho' a man were admitted into Heaven to view the wonderful fabrick of the world, and the beauty of the stars, yet what would otherwise be rapture and extasie, would be but melancholy amazement if he had not a friend to communicate it to.' (Even if you could see the world from the heavens, and the stars, it would not be a pleasure without having a friend to tell about it.)

Start at 'You' read down to the top of the head, left side of head, left eye starting at 'solvers', right eye starting at 'You', right side of head, bottom of head, down neck, up left arm and down right, then down body.

Well on Our Way

Philip Waddell

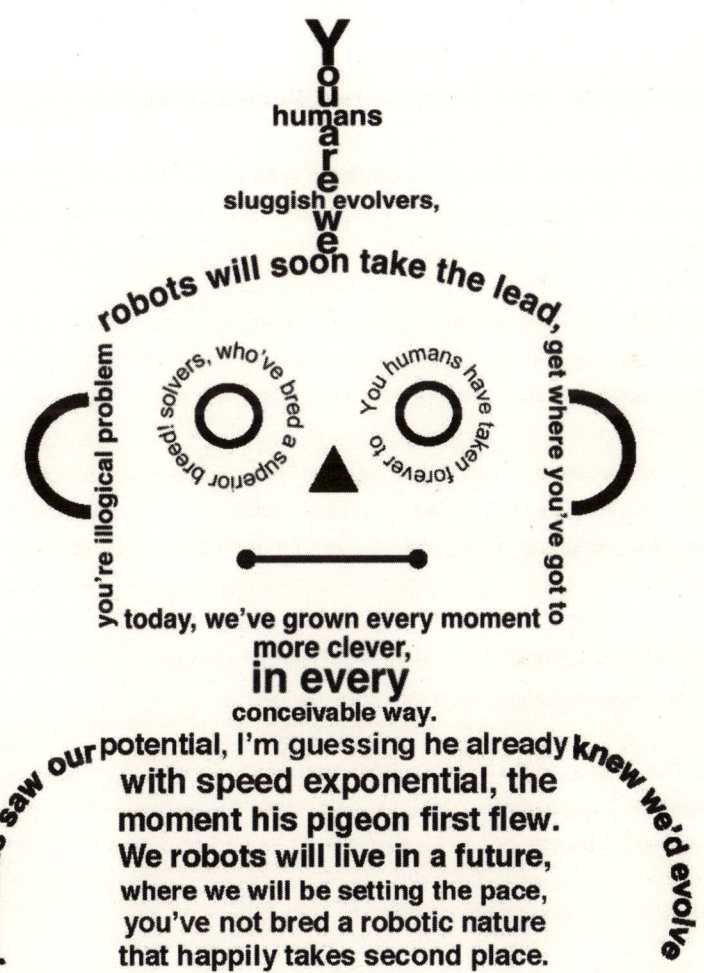

You humans are sluggish evolvers,
we robots will soon take the lead,
you're illogical problem solvers,
who've bred a superior breed!
You humans have taken forever to
get where you've got to today,
we've grown every moment more clever,
in every conceivable way.
Archytas saw our potential, I'm guessing he already knew we'd evolve
with speed exponential, the
moment his pigeon first flew.
We robots will live in a future,
where we will be setting the pace,
you've not bred a robotic nature
that happily takes second place.

Otto F. Rohwedder, 1880–1960, Invented the Bread-Slicing Machine

In 1880, Otto Frederick Rohwedder was born in Iowa, the United States. He went to public schools, was apprenticed to a jeweller to learn a trade, and also studied and graduated with a degree in optics.

FAMOUS FOR: After graduating, Rohwedder worked hard and became the owner of three jewellery stores. He began using his knowledge and skills learned while working with metals and watch mechanisms. He became determined to design a bread-slicing machine.

He sold his jewellery stores to get the money to develop and manufacture his idea. Eventually he patented a machine that sliced and wrapped bread. He sold it to a baker, and the first sliced, wrapped loaf was sold in 1928.

FASCINATING FACT: In 1928, housework was much harder – vacuums were not effective. Hardly anyone had a washing machine. Any invention that saved time was very welcome! Nowadays, most bread sold is sliced.

QUOTE: The saying, 'it's the greatest thing since sliced bread' is probably based on the first advertising slogan for sliced bread. It said: 'the greatest forward step in the baking industry since bread was wrapped'.

Start reading the piece of bread at 'It's hard', read round to 'up', then read round the plate starting at 'some'.

The Man Who Used His Loaf

Shauna Darling Robertson

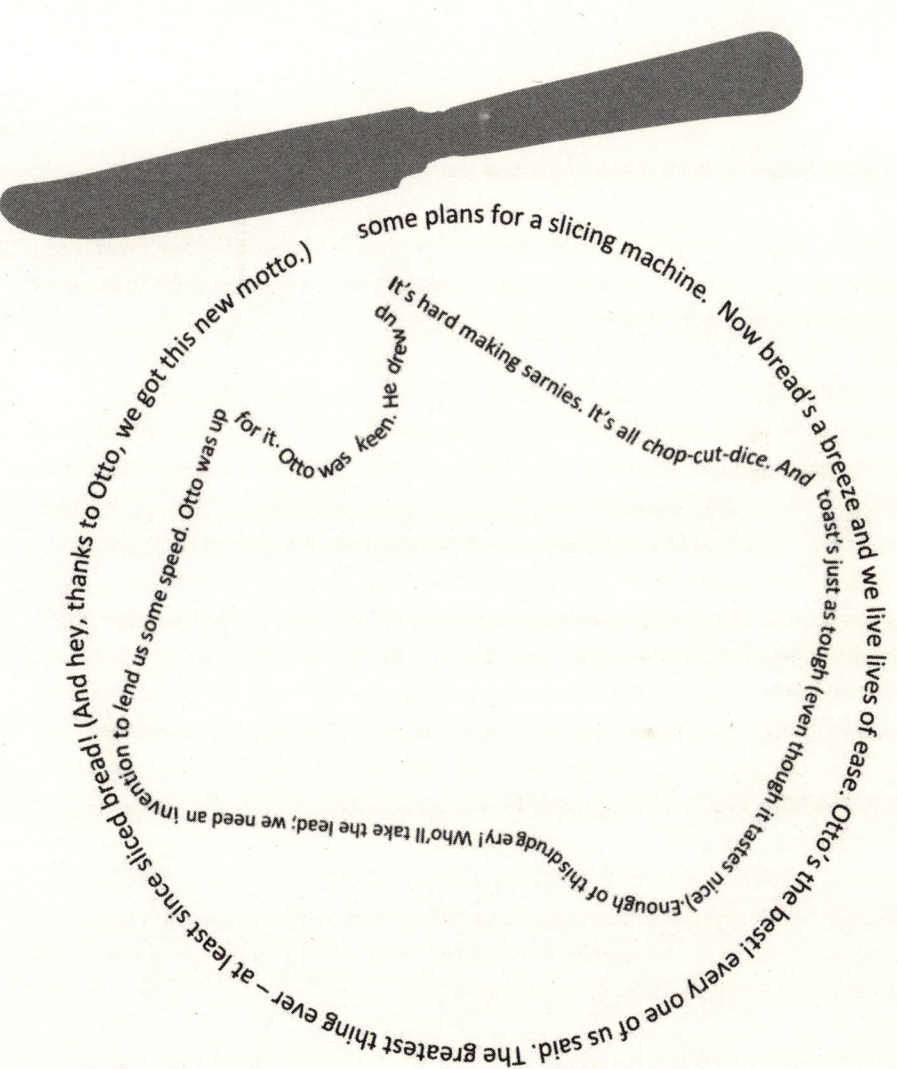

It's hard making sarnies. It's all chop-cut-dice. And
toast's just as tough (even though it tastes nice).
Enough of this drudgery! Who'll take the lead;
we need an invention to lend us some speed.
Otto was up for it. Otto was keen.
He drew up some plans for a slicing machine.
Now bread's a breeze and we live lives of ease.
Otto's the best! every one of us said.
The greatest thing ever – at least since sliced bread!
(And hey, thanks to Otto, we got this new motto.)

John Logie Baird, 1888–1946, Invented the First Working Television

In 1930, John Logie Baird televised the very first drama for the BBC. Baird was born in Helensburgh, Scotland. As a teenager he became very interested in electronics and went on to study electrical engineering.

FAMOUS FOR: In his twenties Baird invented many things that were not very successful. His glass razors shattered, and his skin cream was too painful to use. He became fascinated by experiments to transmit moving pictures and sound. After many setbacks, he managed to transmit an image of a dummy's head. In 1926, he showed a clear moving image of a person. His audience were some scientists and a reporter from *The Times* newspaper.

Baird set up the Baird Television Development Company in 1928. He made the very first drama programme called *The Man with the Flower in His Mouth*, for the BBC. However the BBC eventually moved over to another system, as Baird's cameras were too complicated. They were also large, heavy, and could not be moved easily.

FASCINATING FACT: As a boy, Baird made a telephone exchange in his bedroom. He was connected to his friends across the street.

QUOTE: 'The image of the dummy's head formed itself on the screen with what appeared to me an almost unbelievable clarity. I had got it! I could scarcely believe my eyes and felt myself shaking with excitement.'

Start reading left to right from the top of the television.

John Logie Baird

Matt Goodfellow

John Logie Baird

John Logie Baird

John Logie Baird was a man not scared,
failures never mattered, though his new
cream had made him
scream and sharp, glass
razors shat- tered. He
scratched his chin and
knew he'd win with an idea most supreme;
to capture moving images of people on
a screen. He set to work and did not
shirk, which proved a shrewd
decision, the world was stunned when
he turned on, his working television!

Benjamin Franklin, 1706—1790, Showed that Lightning is Electricity

In 1752, Benjamin Franklin performed a daring experiment to show that lightning is electricity. His parents were very poor when he was born in Massachusetts, the United States. Franklin only went to school until he was ten years old. He learned things by reading until he was a polymath – an expert in many things!

FAMOUS FOR: Franklin is best known as one of the Founding Fathers of the United States. They helped lead the War of Independence from the United Kingdom. He was a writer and newspaper owner. He experimented at cooling things by evaporation, and studied ocean currents. Among other things he invented are a glass musical instrument, a stove and bifocal glasses.

Famously, Franklin demonstrated that lightning was electricity by flying a kite during an electrical storm. He extracted sparks from a cloud. To prevent himself getting an electric shock, he stood on an insulating material. This experiment led to his invention of the lightning rod, to protect buildings being struck by lightning.

FASCINATING FACT: Franklin didn't just use kites during his lightning experiments, he also used them to pull boats and people across water. He was an early windsurfer!

QUOTE: 'By failing to prepare, you are preparing to fail.'

Start at the top.

The Kite Experiment

Suzy Levinson

A
metal
key, a silken kite,
a length of wire, a stormy night.
A Leyden jar, a wetted
string, electric fire...
a lightning
zing
!
His mind unlocked a shocking thing!

Thomas Edison, 1847–1931, Produced the First Practical Electric Light

In 1880, Edison patented the first practical light bulb. A patent is a certificate which says a design is yours and no one else can manufacture it. Thomas Alva Edison was born in Ohio in the United States. He was taught at home by his mother.

FAMOUS FOR: Edison's first job was selling sweets and newspapers on trains. Then he saved the station agent's three-year-old son from a runaway train. The agent trained him to be a telegraph operator. This job taught him the basics of electricity.

Edison kept on studying, did experiments and invented many things. In 1880, after many trials, he invented a working light bulb that could be mass-produced. He brought light indoors. Like an electrical current, Edison was always full of energy. He called failures 'ways of not working' and kept trying. Eventually he had 1,093 patents for his inventions. They included devices for sound recording and motion pictures. He became famous all over the world.

FASCINATING FACT: When Edison was a child he sat on a clutch of his neighbour's goose eggs to see if they would hatch.

QUOTES: 'Genius is one per cent inspiration and ninety-nine per cent perspiration.'

'The reason a lot of people do not recognize opportunity is because it usually goes around wearing overalls looking like hard work.'

Start at 'When' on the left side of the bulb, read round, then start inside with the filament at 'fish line' and read round, then read the bottom.

A Light-Bulb Moment

Chrissie Gittins

When you are reaching in the dark for the light switch, think of Edison. When you see a shop lit up at night, think of Edison. When you read by a lamp before sleep, think of Edison. He tried thousands of ways to make a light bulb filament;

fish line, copper, platinum, six thousand slivers of plants - oak, fern, spruce. When he discovered that elecricity would glow through bamboo for fifty days his delight shone bright. Edison - not the first to make a light bulb but

the first to make a
light bulb last. He
pushed glorious
light into night.

Ludwig van Beethoven, 1770–1827, Composed Modern Classical Music

In 1795, Ludwig van Beethoven wrote his first piece of music for public performance. He was born in Bonn, Germany. His father, who was a musician and teacher, taught him music – he beat him to make him practise hard. Aged twenty-one, Beethoven left home and went to study composing music with the famous composer, Joseph Haydn.

FAMOUS FOR: By the age of twenty-five, Beethoven was an outstanding pianist. His first public performance piece displayed a new style of composing. People loved his beautiful cantatas, written for a person or choir to sing with musical instruments. He soon became famous. One of his best-known works is called Moonlight Sonata.

Sadly Beethoven began to lose his hearing – he was almost completely deaf by the age of forty-one. He had to stop performing, but carried on composing. Amazingly the bulk of Beethoven's most admired works were completed during this time.

FASCINATING FACT: Beethoven had to leave school aged eleven to help his family. He never learned to multiply or divide. He always wrote out 60 x 60 as sixty 60s, to add them up!

QUOTE: 'What I have in my heart and soul – must find a way out. That's the reason for music.'

Start at the moon 'Ludwig' and then read the waves left to right.

Beethoven

Roger Stevens

Ludwig

configures a tune
that will move the emotions
of millions of lovers and friends - a dark sky cantata;
watch the ripples and shimmers of stars on the lake
as they dance in the magical night of the Moonlight Sonata

William Wordsworth, 1770–1850, English Romantic Poet

In 1770, William Wordsworth, the celebrated poet, was born in Cockermouth, England. He was particularly close to his younger sister Dorothy. Wordsworth's father encouraged him to read, and to learn poems by poets such as Shakespeare off by heart. He came to love nature and the moors where he lived.

FAMOUS FOR: Wordsworth wrote one of the most well-known poems: 'I Wandered Lonely as a Cloud', sometimes called 'Daffodils'. He helped introduce a new style of poetry called Romanticism. It focused on emotion and love of nature. When he and Samuel Coleridge wrote their famous poetry book, *Lyrical Ballads,* Wordsworth tried to use everyday language that everyone could enjoy.

Wordsworth and his wife Mary lived with his sister Dorothy in Dove Cottage in the Lake District, where he wrote many of his most famous poems. He believed that a poet uses their imagination to transform poetry from the ordinary, and show deep truths.

FASCINATING FACTS: Dove Cottage is now a 'writer's home museum'. The poet Gerard Benson wrote this poem after visiting and reading one of Wordsworth's manuscripts, which his sister Dorothy and wife Mary used to write out by hand. Vellum was a type of animal skin used to write on. Recto and verso mean the writing on the front and back of a piece of paper. Fascicles can mean a bundle of thin leaves.

QUOTE: 'Poetry is the spontaneous overflow of powerful feelings: it takes its origin from emotion recollected in tranquillity.'

Start at the top of the feather pen, read downwards left to right and then read the ink bottle left to right.

Dove Cottage Manuscript 44

Gerard Benson

Holding
it in
my hands,
trying its weight,
the thick,
small book,
I feel a
thump
and throb
of blood
against my
temples.
The copied
poems, page
after page
covered
with deft,
neat

writing, *verso* and
recto, detonate silently
inside me, a time bomb
fused by those women,
in the slow, long days of
labour, filling the homemade
fascicles with glowing odes and sonnets -
There was a time ... The world is too much with
us ... Nuns Fret not (nor, it seem, sisters and wives,
the copyists): and more - set firm across their
graceful loops, an uglier, darker hand,
Wordsworth's, correcting. This
vellum enfolds lives.

Albert Einstein, 1879–1955, The World's Most Brilliant Scientist

In 1915, Albert Einstein explained his theory of relativity. One of the cleverest and most inventive scientists the world has seen, he was born in Ulm, Germany, and emigrated to the United States. Although skilled at maths from an early age, he didn't speak until he was four years old! When Einstein was five, his interest in science was sparked by being given a pocket compass by his father. He said that watching the compass needle move when he was a boy made him feel that 'something deeply hidden had to be behind things'.

FAMOUS FOR: Einstein's theory of relativity explained many things that puzzled scientists. One thing relativity states is that speed of motion is always relative to something else. Imagine being on a train, and throwing a ball in the direction the train is travelling. The ball would move quite slowly to you. But think of someone outside watching the train pass. To them, the ball is travelling at the speed of the train, plus its own speed.

Einstein's theories about space, time and matter (anything you can touch) changed the way scientists thought about energy. He provided lots of ways to advance technology, both good and bad – enabling both travel to the moon, and atomic bombs.

FASCINATING FACTS: Einstein was famous for his mad hairstyle (which he never combed), and for not wearing any socks. At the age of twelve, Einstein taught himself algebra and geometry over a single summer.

QUOTE: 'The true sign of intelligence is not knowledge but imagination.'

Start in the middle of the spiral and read outwards.

Albert at the Beach

Mark Hoadley

It was my birthday. I was five. I remember a red balloon. We were at the beach. Mama, Papa, Maja and me. Papa gave me a pocket compass. Maja slept. Mama stretched in pantaloons. There are two Alberts in my class. Albert M and Albert E. I am not Albert M. It's my birthday. I'm five. I stare and stare at the compass hands. Maja sleeps. Mama twirls in her favourite pantaloons. Papa hums a sweet tune. I stare and stare at the compass hands. They spin around like a magic thing. Papa hums a sweet, sad tune. I follow the compass hands from dune to dune. They spin around like a magic thing. Or is it me that spins? I follow those hands from dune to dune: North, East, South, West! We're at the beach. It's my birthday. I'm Albert E not Albert M. Maja sleeps. Mama twirls. Papa hums the saddest tune. And there's a red (or is it blue?) balloon.

Beatrice Tinsley, 1941–1981, Proved the Universe is Expanding

In 1966, Beatrice Tinsley completed her PhD thesis and changed how scientists understand the universe. Born Beatrice Muriel Hill in Chester, England, she emigrated to New Zealand with her family. Later she emigrated to the United States with her husband.

FAMOUS FOR: Tinsley became a doctor of astrophysics at the University of Texas. She was so clever she did it in two years, instead of the six it takes most people. What she wrote for her degree showed how galaxies are formed and age. It explained the universe has no boundaries and will expand forever. She has been compared to Einstein for her research.

Tinsley found that because she was a woman, it was hard to be taken seriously as a scientist in Texas. Determined to use her extraordinary brain to study the universe, she applied for jobs elsewhere. She became the first female astronomy professor at Yale University. To do this, she had to get divorced and leave her children, as a married woman could not hold such a post.

FASCINATING FACTS: As a child, she was called 'Beetle' by her friends and family. She loved to play the violin; and was only forty years old when she died.

QUOTE: 'To be rejected and undervalued intellectually is a gut problem to me . . .'

Start in the middle at 'I', then go on to 'began' and read around in a circle spiral to the outside. It's easier than it looks!

Expanding Forever

Elena de Roo

wherever you

from stand

endless growing

only for

away open there

my is the

stretch to now began no red

shift

I limits bang **I** with stopping

as or big no of

a an

slowing

edge or end no

centre forever infinite where

galactic

expanding band elastic

my

you

are

always is

Ravi Shankar, 1920–2012, Influenced the Beatles and Western Music

In 1920, Rabindro Shaunkar Chowdhury was born in Varanasi, India. Known later as Ravi Shankar, he toured India when he was only ten years old with his famous brother Uday's dance group. He learned to dance and play Indian musical instruments.

FAMOUS FOR: Shankar's amazing ability led him to be trained by music masters. He became a superb musician and his compositions and performances united both Eastern and Western music. His most famous piece of music is Concerto for Sitar and Orchestra. He also composed music for ballets and became a musical director for the record label HMV India.

During the sixties and seventies he toured the world. The Beatle George Harrison heard him play. Shankar gave him sitar lessons and Harrison used the instrument on a famous Beatles' track, 'Norwegian Wood'.

FASCINATING FACT: Ravi Shankar was made an Honorary Knight Commander of the Order of the British Empire. Queen Elizabeth presented him with the award in 2001 for his services to music.

QUOTE: 'Dream the impossible. Know that you are born in this world to do something wonderful and unique; don't let this opportunity pass by. Give yourself the freedom to dream and think big.'

Start at the top and read left to right down every line to the bottom.

Ravi Shankar

Penny Kent

His
fingers
blurred,
they
flew so fast
and crawled
among the frets.
His sitar
sprinkled
falling
stars
and
growled
low, sad
regrets.
His
fingers
stretched
the sitar
strings and
plucked ins- piring
snaps. His sitar chimed
with jangling twangs
and danced with tabla taps.
His music soared from India
and the Beatles swelled
his fame. His sitar spun new
ragas - Ravi Shankar was
his name.

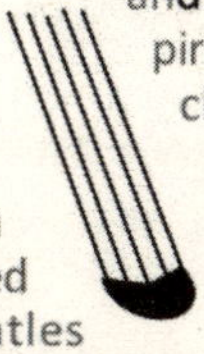

Sir Isaac Newton, 1642–1727, First Described the Force of Gravity

In 1687, Sir Isaac Newton described his theory of gravity. Newton was born on a farm in Woolsthorpe-by-Colsterworth, England. Sadly, his father died three months before he was born. He went to Cambridge University and later taught there.

FAMOUS FOR: There is a story about how Isaac Newton came up with his theory about gravity. He saw an apple fall from a tree, and wondered why it fell to the ground, and didn't go upwards or sideways. His theory was there must be a force in everything, that pulls towards itself. The bigger the object, the bigger the force would be. So the tiny apple with a tiny force would be overcome by the Earth's large force. He named this force gravity.

Among other accomplishments, he explained the nature of light and colour. He invented a telescope on which today's Newton telescopes are based.

FASCINATING FACTS: Isaac Newton was knighted by Queen Anne in 1705. The world's most valuable tooth is thought to have belonged to him – it was sold in 1816 for £730, which nowadays would be more than £25,000.

QUOTE: 'We build too many walls and not enough bridges.'

Start at the top and read to the bottom of the apple.

A Bash of Inspiration

Kate Williams

When
a rosy apple fell on his head,
this young thinker sprang up and
said: *Gravity caused that fruit to fall!*
(The bump didn't faze the fellow at all.)
Everyone knows, you know and I, that
apples will fall – not rise to the sky!
But when this one dropped down
from the tree, it proved his
theory of gravity.

John Muir, 1838–1914, Preserved Nature in American National Parks

In 1890, John Muir helped establish Yosemite National Park in California, the United States. Muir was born in Dunbar, Scotland, and emigrated to the United States with his family when he was eleven years old. There, he had to work very hard on his father's farm. In his breaks, he became fascinated with the natural world.

FAMOUS FOR: After university, Muir went to work in a factory, where he had an accident that blinded him for a few weeks. This changed his life – he decided to follow his real love. What he wanted to do was travel through the unexplored beauty of nature.

Muir walked a thousand miles through the Florida swamps to the Gulf of Mexico. He decided to go the 'wildest, leafiest, and least trodden way I could find'. He wrote about conserving nature on this journey and others. This led to the establishment of National Parks, including Yosemite and the Grand Canyon – both preserved by John Muir's inspiring writing.

FASCINATING FACTS: As well as becoming known as 'The Father of the National Parks', Muir was a talented wood carver. When he was young he made curious mechanical inventions, such a bed that tipped him out just before dawn.

QUOTE: 'Nature is ever at work building and pulling down, creating and destroying, keeping everything whirling and flowing, allowing no rest but in rhythmical motion, chasing everything in endless song out of one beautiful form into another.'

Start at 'Flat' and read each left branch followed by each right branch on each line.

Flat spot found under the trees
soft floor of sun warmed needles,
pine-bough bed. He unrolls a cloth
from his pack and lies down,
settles into the hold of the earth, the ground
the voice of the river is a distant song
and the moon in the trees his companion till dawn.

JOHN MUIR

Valentina Tereshkova, born 1937, First Woman in Space

In 1963, Valentina Tereshkova became the first woman to fly into space. She was born in a village, Maslennikovo, in Russia. Her father was a tractor driver, then a tank driver in the Russian army. He died when she was two years old. Valentina was brought up by her mother and became interested in parachuting when she was young.

FAMOUS FOR: After leaving school, Tereshkova continued her education while working. She also trained in skydiving, and then as a competitive parachutist. The Russian director of cosmonaut training learned that America was preparing women astronauts. He became determined that Russia would be the first to send women to space. Four hundred women were selected to be considered. Valentina Tereshkova became one of five women to start training.

On the 16 June 1963, at the age of twenty-six, Valentina Tereshkova became the first woman in space. She remains the youngest woman in space, and the only woman to pilot a spacecraft alone. Her call sign was 'chaika' which means seagull.

FASCINATING FACT: Tereshkova's favourite planet is Mars and she has said she is ready to fly there even if there is no flight back.

QUOTE: 'It is me, Seagull! Everything is fine. I see the horizon; it's a sky blue with a dark strip. How beautiful the Earth is . . . everything is going well'.

Start at the top and read left to right all the way down, then the left-hand side rocket trail then the right-hand side rocket trail.

Chaika

Myles McLeod

Chaika,
Valentina Tereshkova,
flew her Vostok module over
Earth in June of sixty-three. When
she launched, she said with glee, 'Hey
sky, take off your hat, I'm coming.' (Or
if you'd like your Russian true: 'Yey,
nyeba, snimi shlyapu, ya idoo.') And
so, the seagull soared, stargazing.
Three days, forty-eight orbits
later, she drove her rocket
back to vapour. Her dad had
driven tractors, later tanks. So
never saw his Vladirmirinovna
thanked with a Soviet outburst
for being the first woman in
space. Hero. Ace. Years later
missions to Mars are
mooted, and Valentina
says she'll be
booted,
suited.
And take a one-way cosmo-climb
to be the first a second time.

Amelia Earhart, 1897–1937, First Woman to Fly Across the Atlantic Ocean

In 1928, Amelia Earhart started her career by being the first woman to fly across the Atlantic as a passenger, and became famous. Earhart was born in Kansas, the United States. She and her sister had lots of freedom as their mother did not believe in bringing up 'nice little girls'. After seeing an air-display team Earhart decided she wanted to fly. She built a roller coaster and flew off her shed roof!

FAMOUS FOR: Between 1930 and 1935, amazingly, she set seven women's aviation records. In 1932, the incredibly brave and pioneering Earhart became the first person to fly solo on a non-stop transatlantic flight, and she received a United States Distinguished Flying Cross. While she was trying to fly around the world in 1937, she disappeared. Her plane went down somewhere in the Pacific Ocean. The mystery of what happened to her is still unsolved to this day.

FASCINATING FACTS: Although Earhart drank hot chocolate while flying, she didn't like coffee or tea. To stay awake on long flights she used smelling salts! These were very unpleasant-smelling and usually used to bring people round after fainting. Earhart supported women's equal rights.

QUOTE: 'Some of us have great runways already built for us. If you have one, take off. But if you don't have one, realize it is your responsibility to grab a shovel and build one for yourself, and for those who will follow after you.'

Read the top wing to 'streaming', then the top tail line, back to the wing and across to the tail left to right all the way down to 'maiden' then left to right from the plane's landing gear to the wing, then to the end.

Amelia Earhart

Sue Hardy-Dawson

Even then,
you were
the leader -
climbing trees.
hair streaming.
belly-slamming
No one minds,
posy we pick
a pet of a tree toad, moths, katydids or that
with the help of a willing uncle, you plan a homemade ramp, cobble together, secure
roof of the old tool shed, ready to launch
our own rollercoaster. You, after its maiden
flight,
wearing
dress,

Winters
downhill.
instead of a
worms, make
it to the

lips bruised, elated,
the medal of a torn
splinters of the
box that served
as a sled,

"Oh, Pidge, it's just like flying!" you said..."

Sir Francis Drake, c. 1541–1596, Defeated the Spanish Armada

In around 1541, English explorer Sir Francis Drake, was born in Tavistock, England. No one is completely sure of the exact dates he was born and died. When his family moved to Kent, he was apprenticed to the owner of a sailing ship aged ten. When the master he was working for died, having had no wife or children, he left his ships to Drake.

FAMOUS FOR: Francis Drake was adventurous, loyal and fearless. He was the second person to sail around the world. He claimed California, in the United States, for Queen Elizabeth the First (who knighted him). He defeated the Spanish Armada – this was a fierce group of Spanish ships sent to defeat the English.

Along with his triumphs, Drake took part in what are now known to be dishonourable activities. He was involved in trading enslaved people and plundering Spanish ships. This was sometimes funded by the British government. The Spanish called him 'El Draque', which means 'The Dragon'.

FASCINATING FACT: Sir Francis Drake is known for finishing a game of bowls before setting out to defeat the Spanish Armada. He was waiting for the weather to improve.

QUOTE: 'There is plenty of time to finish this game, and to thrash the Spaniards, too.'

Start at 'He gave' and read left to right from top to bottom.

El Draque

Sue Hardy-Dawson

He gave

her silver, a
Spaniard's

gold, begged
he might sail
around the

globe. He took to
the waves and
he dared to dream

of bringing the world to his Faerie
Queen. They told him of dragons in tales
of old, of sirens, that drowned those who
came too close. Yet he heard no voice
but the song of the sea, saw only the
smile of his Faerie Queen. He sailed
from the Northern lands so cold, sallied

due
South as he pitched and
rolled. He looked to the West, then to the
East and he gave what he found to his
Faerie Queen. So when the Armada
came in too close, it's said he waited
to finish his bowls, then saved Merry
England for you and me, and all for
the love of his Faerie Queen.

Junko Tabei, 1939–2016, First Woman to Climb Mount Everest

In 1975, Junko Tabei was the first woman to climb Mount Everest. Born in Fukushima, Japan, Ishibashi Junko first became interested in climbing on a school trip. (In Japan, your surname comes before your given name.)

FAMOUS FOR: When she was at Showa Women's University, Tabei met a group of male mountaineers. This group did not take her seriously as a climber because she was a woman. They were reluctant to climb with her. So in 1969 she formed her own women's mountain climbing group, the Ladies Climbing Club: Japan. Their slogan was 'Let's go on an overseas expedition by ourselves'. By 1972, Tabei had successfully climbed many mountains, such as Mount Fuji and the Matterhorn. She was now recognised as a serious mountaineer.

When Tabei wanted to climb Mount Everest, most of her team were women. They had difficulties getting sponsorship money for an expedition, but finally a newspaper provided funding. Junko Tabei succeeded in reaching the summit of Everest with her Sherpa guide, Ang Tsering.

FASCINATING FACT: Twelve days before they reached the top of Everest, Tabei's team were hit by an avalanche. She was buried and knocked out for six minutes until her Sherpa guide dug her out.

QUOTE: 'Technique and ability alone do not get you to the top; it is the willpower that is the most important. This willpower you cannot buy with money or be given by others . . . it rises from your heart.'

Start at the bottom at 'Ignore' and read the lines left to right up to the top.

The Climb

Sam Cummings

top.
reach the
stop. You'll
drop, but do not
down you may
and tumble. Down,
ignore the fear of toss
slide's roar and rumble,
others said. Ignore the snow
your head. Ignore the lies the
bones. Ignore the doubts within
Ignore the cold that gnaws your
Ignore the wind that howls and moans.

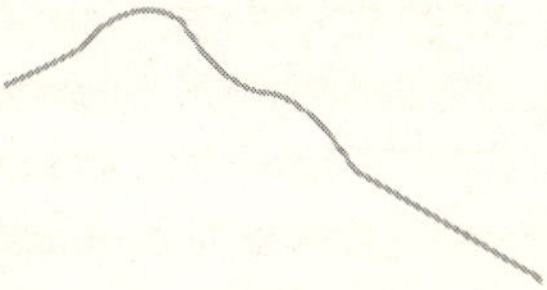

Start

Rachel Carson, 1907–1964, Inspired the U.S. Environmental Movement

In 1962, Rachel Carson's famous book, *Silent Spring* was published. Carson was born in Pennsylvania, the United States, on a farm. She enjoyed learning about animals and reading and writing from a young age. At university she studied biology.

FAMOUS FOR: Carson became a marine biologist. Her first book, *Under the Sea Wind,* contained stories about sea creatures, using real facts. Her second book, *The Sea Around Us,* was a best-seller.

However her most famous book was *Silent Spring.* It warned that pesticides would not just kill pest animals, but other creatures too. She foresaw it would also affect insects needed to pollinate crops. Carson said one day we risked awakening to a silent spring, with no birds or insects. This book aided in the banning of the harmful chemical DDT, and helped support the world's environmental movements.

FASCINATING FACT: Rachel Carson had her first writing published in a magazine aged ten.

QUOTE: 'Over increasingly large areas of the United States, spring now comes unheralded by the return of the birds, and the early mornings are strangely silent where once they were filled with the beauty of birdsong.'

Start at 'Inside the empty flower' – the poem is written in black at the bottom.

Rachel Carson

Liz Brownlee

Inside the empty flower was no bee, no bee sipping no nectar, bathing in no pollen. No
petal trembled or lifted as no bee flew. No bee was silent, like no bird on no branch above.
Inside the empty flower was no bee, no bee sipping no nectar, bathing in no pollen. No
petal trembled or lifted as no bee flew. No bee was silent, like no bird on no branch above.
Inside the empty flower was no e sipping no nectar, bathing in no pollen. No
petal trembled or lifted as no b was silent, like no bird on no branch above.
Inside the empty flower was n pping no nectar, bathing in no pollen. No
petal trembled or o b was no bird on no branch above.
Inside the emp o s r, bathing in no pollen. No
petal trembled bird on no branch above.
Inside the emp r, bathing in no pollen. No
petal trembled o no bird on no branch above.
Inside the empty flower w ing no nectar, bathing in no pollen. No
petal trembled or lifte lent, like no bird on no branch above.
Inside the empty fl o nectar, bathing in no pollen. No
petal trembled or li , like no bird on no branch above.
Inside the empty fl e, n nectar, bathing in no pollen. No
petal trembled or lift flew. N nt, like no bird on no branch above.
Inside the empty flower was no bee, no be g no nectar, bathing in no pollen. No
petal trembled or lifted as no bee flew. No bee was silent, like no bird on no branch above.
Inside the empty flower was no bee, no bee sipping no nectar, bathing in no pollen. No
petal trembled or lifted as no bee flew. No bee was silent, like no bird on no branch above.
Inside the empty flower was no bee, no bee sipping no nectar, bathing in no pollen. No
petal trembled or lifted as no bee flew. No bee was silent, like no bird on no branch above.
Inside the empty flower was no bee, no bee sipping no nectar, bathing in no pollen. No
petal trembled or lifted as no bee flew. No bee was silent, like no bird on no branch above.
Inside the empty flower was no bee, no bee sipping no nectar, bathing in no pollen. No
petal trembled or lifted as no bee flew. No bee was silent, like no bird on no branch above.
Inside the empty flower was no bee, no bee sipping no nectar, bathing in no pollen. No
petal trembled or lifted as no bee flew. No bee was silent, like no bird on no branch above.
Inside the empty flower was no bee, no bee sipping no nectar, bathing in no pollen. No
petal trembled or lifted as no bee flew. No bee was silent, like no bird on no branch above.
**Inside the empty flower was no bee, no bee sipping no nectar, bathing in no pollen. No
petal trembled or lifted as no bee flew. No bee was silent, like no bird on no branch above.**

Maya Angelou, 1928–2014, Award-Winning Influential Author and Civil Rights Activist

In 2000, Maya Angelou was presented with the United States National Medal of Arts. She was born Marguerite Annie Johnson in Missouri, the United States. Her older brother called her 'Mya' for 'Mya little sister'.

FAMOUS FOR: Angelou had an unsettled childhood, and when she was eight, her mother's boyfriend attacked her. She told her brother, who told her uncles. The man was jailed, let out after only one day, and was murdered soon after. Angelou blamed herself. She did not speak again for five years. When she was at school, a teacher showed her books by Charles Dickens and Black female authors such as Frances Harper and they influenced her later life and career. This teacher gradually helped her to speak again.

Angelou led a mixed and extraordinary life. She worked as a cable car driver, and became a campaigner for Black civil rights. She was also a talented film director, singer, public speaker and poet. Her award-winning book is called *I Know Why the Caged Bird Sings*, and is the first of seven autobiographies for which she is best known.

FASCINATING FACTS: Maya Angelou received more than fifty honorary degrees in her lifetime. She recited her poem 'On the Pulse of Morning' at President Clinton's inauguration as President of the United States in 1993.

QUOTE: 'I've learned that people will forget what you said, people will forget what you did, but people will never forget how you made them feel.'

Start at the bird's head, then read each line left to right across the left and right wings, then left to right down the tail.

Hope She Shouts

Jan Dean

No
cage
could
hold
this burning bird, bright with
songs to set the world alight, whose diamond words
will wing and shine through dust
she is her voice, rich and honey-dark and sweet
strong as the pillars of earth
she stands outlasting those who stand
for ill, alive in every word she
wrote, each syllable a footbeat heartbeat
drumdance power.
Love she shouts
find the tool
that fits your hand
and work a
wonder in the world
by loving it
against all odds
you are enough, she says.

Samuel Johnson, 1709–1784, Wrote the First Comprehensive Dictionary

In 1755, Samuel Johnson published his famous Dictionary of the English Language. Johnson was born in Lichfield, England. He went to Oxford University, but had to leave because his parents couldn't afford the fees.

FAMOUS FOR: Johnson started work writing articles for a newspaper. He did not earn much, but continued writing in many areas. He could translate work from Latin and Greek, write poetry, and novels. These literary achievements impressed publishers. Eventually, in 1747, a group of them asked him to write a dictionary.

The dictionary took eight years to write. Walter Jackson Bate was a critic at the time (a literary critic studies books and let's others know their opinion of it). He said the dictionary: 'easily ranks as one of the greatest single achievements of scholarship . . .' There were no computers. Johnson had to find the words in letters, documents and libraries of books. He wrote a description to explain each word, included many in quotations, and some were also illustrated.

FASCINATING FACT: The dictionary was 46cm tall and 51cm thick, and contained 42,773 entries. In today's money, it would cost £350. The equivalent first French dictionary took fifty-five years and forty scholars to write!

QUOTES: 'The greatest part of a writer's time is spent in reading, in order to write: a man will turn over half a library to make one book.'

'A writer only begins a book. A reader finishes it.'

Start at 'Samuel' and read left to right from top to bottom.

Samuel Johnson's Dictionary of the English Language

Stewart Ennis

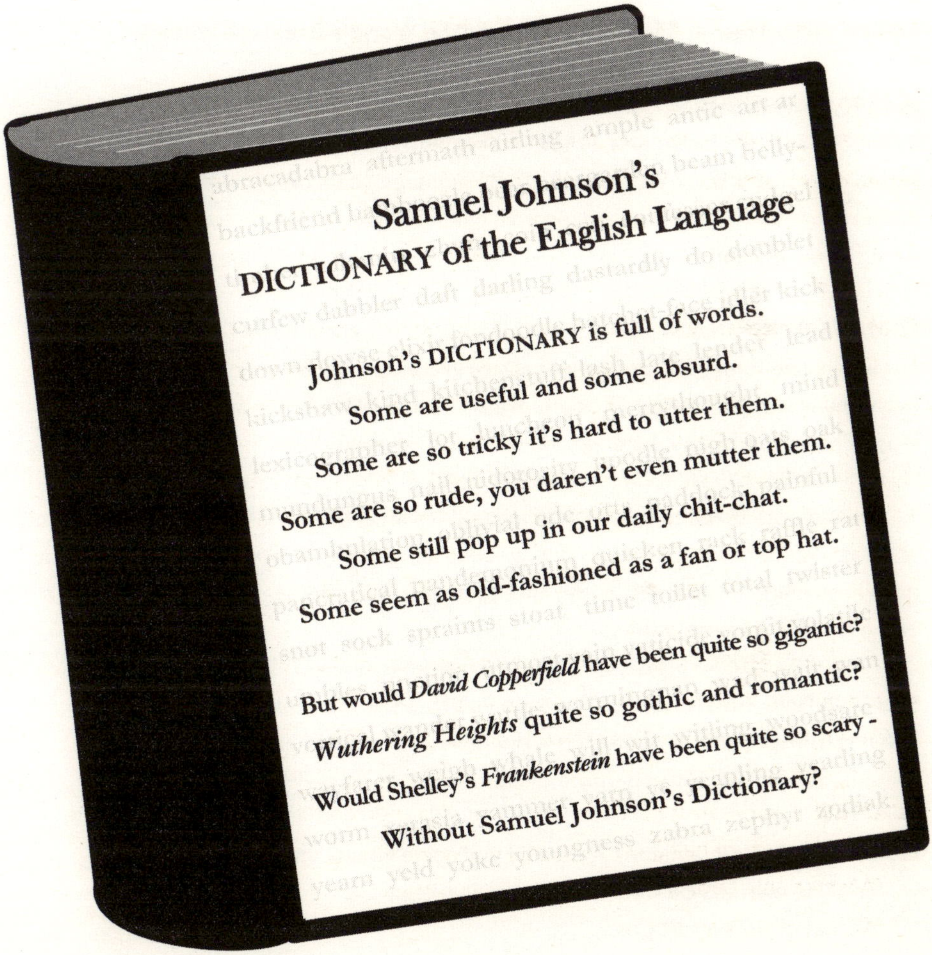
Samuel Johnson's
DICTIONARY of the English Language
Johnson's DICTIONARY is full of words.
Some are useful and some absurd.
Some are so tricky it's hard to utter them.
Some are so rude, you daren't even mutter them.
Some still pop up in our daily chit-chat.
Some seem as old-fashioned as a fan or top hat.
But would *David Copperfield* have been quite so gigantic?
Wuthering Heights quite so gothic and romantic?
Would Shelley's *Frankenstein* have been quite so scary -
Without Samuel Johnson's Dictionary?

William Shakespeare, 1564–1616, One of the World's Greatest Writers

In 1590, William Shakespeare wrote his first play. He was born in Stratford-Upon-Avon, England. His father was a glove maker, and probably had the money to send him to grammar school. When he was only eighteen years old, Shakespeare married Anne Hathaway. As there are no records, much of his early life can only be guessed at, so remains a mystery.

FAMOUS FOR: At some point, Shakespeare became known as an actor and playwright. He formed a company of actors in London. When he started writing, he wrote many sonnets, a type of poem. He also wrote plays; comedy plays, and some loosely based on history. Later on, he started to write what are thought his best works, his tragedies. But these too contained humour.

Shakespeare loved to play with language. He invented hundreds of new words and phrases. Before Shakespeare, no one was critical, gloomy or lonely. These new words must have made his plays colourful and exciting to listen to. He is now known as one of the world's greatest writers.

FASCINATING FACT: During Shakespeare's lifetime, many exciting things happened. The first newspaper was printed. The gunpowder plot was foiled, and the Spanish Armada was fought. None of these events appear in his plays.

QUOTES: 'What's in a name? A rose by any name would smell as sweet.'
'To thine own self be true.'
'All that glisters is not gold.'

Start at 'William' and read left to right down the face to 'Prospero's', then start at 'staff' on the outside line of the collar, read around to 'chimney', then start on the inside line of the collar round to 'things', then the inside, and lastly the outside, of the neck line.

Matt Goodfellow

William, I don't think there's much point in me talking about the big things in this poem: the infinite fame of a glover's son, the plaudits, the much squabbled-over amount of invented words, the careful craft of page and stage, the second favourite bed, being born and dying on the same day (also squabbled over), no, I don't think there's much point in talking about these things – it's been done many times before by far more skilled writers than me. So let me talk instead about the little things, the things you mean to me: the bite of acid on my lips when I read Iago's words aloud for the first time, the tears on Miss Jones' cheek when we acted out the death scenes of Romeo and Juliet, how you made me want to break down the walls of my stuffy classroom and find the sounds and sweet airs of Caliban's Isle, hold Prospero's staff aloft beneath swirling, purple skies, Granpa's small smile as he whispered golden lads and girls all must, as chimney sweepers, come to dust, at Gramma's funeral, Yes, I think these things explain it better, these small things, to put it simply as I can, you're my guiding star - my genius.

Ursula Le Guin, 1929–2018, Ground-Breaking Modern Author

In 2000, Ursula Le Guin was named a Living Legend by the United States Library of Congress. This was for making a huge contribution to the cultural heritage (writing of historical importance) of America. She was born Ursula Kroeber in California, the United states. Her parents' house was full of books. As she read, she became a fan of science fiction, fantasy, myths and legends.

FAMOUS FOR: Very few people have received awards for so many types of writing. Le Guin wrote twenty-three adult novels, twelve short story collections, eleven books of poetry, and eight collections of feminist essays. (Feminism is about making sure women and men have equal rights.) The book that made her famous was *The Wizard of Earthsea,* the first of thirteen children's books. It has sold millions of copies worldwide.

The Wizard of Earthsea is a fantasy book for children. It influenced many books written afterwards. Ged, a young boy who shows great power as a child, is trained further at a school of Wizadry. In the book, Ged frees some poor villagers from the threat of dragons.

FASCINATING FACT: Ursula Le Guin started writing aged nine. She sent a short story to *Astounding Science Fiction* when she was eleven, but it was rejected.

QUOTE: 'People who deny the existence of dragons are often eaten by dragons. From within.'

Start at 'She', read to 'and' round the wing, to 'clicks', then second wing to the nose, then from 'electric' to the chin, then left leg down and toes left to right, right leg down and toes left to right, then the top of the tail to the end and the bottom of the tail to the end.

Wizard

Jan Dean

She makes words and mindspit, knows that what
she speaks first rises
in the soft machinery of brain cells, flows through rivers of nerves to
become clicks, sighs of speech, understands the bash of air
molecules thumping against an ear-drum, the pulse of eardrum up into another brain which reads those click
electric ticks as words, as meaning,
all that stuff – the way sound moves, the way it is one
thing that joins the speaker to the listener, she knows that and
so she makes worlds with words and
the sudden explosions of ideas in her head (let's call it mindspit). She does it because it matters that we
join together, it matters that together we imagine how things could be if we were kinder, more human, more like family that we ought to be

Sir John Tenniel, 1820–1914, Illustrated the 'Alice' Books

In 1865, *Alice's Adventures in Wonderland* was published, illustrated by Sir John Tenniel. Tenniel was born in London, England. He was quiet and shy. He trained in sculpture and taught himself illustration. He would draw zoo animals in Regent's Park and go to London theatres to draw actors from the pits.

FAMOUS FOR: Tenniel became an illustrator, and later a cartoonist for *Punch* magazine. *Punch* printed opinions about social conditions of the time. Victorian Britain was becoming more aware of injustice, such as making small children climb up chimneys to clean them. Tenniel's humorous cartoons brought attention to these wrongs. People began to question their acceptance of them. He became famous and people looked forward to reading his cartoons.

The author Lewis Carroll admired his unique and fantastical illustrations. He wanted Tenniel to illustrate his fantasy, *Alice's Adventures in Wonderland*. The pictures Tenniel drew were placed on the page to interact with the text, which had never been done before.

FASCINATING FACT: Tenniel's illustrations were not very well printed in the first edition of *Alice's Adventures in Wonderland.* Lewis Carroll paid to have them printed again.

QUOTE: 'It is a curious fact that with *Through the Looking-Glass* the faculty of making book illustrations departed from me . . . I have done nothing in that direction since.'

Start at 'Who' and read left to right from top to bottom.

Sir John Tenniel

Dom Conlon

Who drew the
grin of an
invisible
cat?

Drink me!

Who
drew the
cost of the maddest hat?
Who drew the tea in a party scene?
Who drew the rage on a red-faced queen?
Who drew the girl from tall to small?
Who drew the grump of an egg on the wall?
Who drew fights of fat, twin boys?
Who drew the jam that a mouse enjoys?
Who drew the tick of a rabbit's clock?
Who drew the burble of a Jabberwock?
Who drew the smoke of an insect's pipe?
Who drew the mushroom nice and ripe?
Who drew the old man upside down?
Who drew the sparkle of a crown?
Who drew the book which
became perennial?

A man by the name of Sir John Tenniel!

Sir Charles Chaplin, 1889–1977, One of the First Comic Actors

In 1940, Charlie Chaplin's most famous film, The Great Dictator, was released. Charles Spencer Chaplin was born in London, England. His father left his mother, and his childhood was spent in extreme poverty. His mother was forced to send Chaplin to a workhouse twice. This was a place for people who had no work and no money. Conditions there were very hard.

FAMOUS FOR: Chaplin began to perform comedy on stage as a way of earning his living. Aged nineteen, he joined a circus group and travelled to the United States. He was noticed by the New York Motion Picture Company, and hired to appear in their films. (In those days films did not have sound. There were organs in cinemas for someone to play exciting or sad music to accompany the films.) For only his second appearance as an actor, Chaplin picked out the famous costume for his sad character, 'The Tramp', who ended up in many hilarious situations.

Chaplin eventually went on to star in most of his films. He also wrote, directed, produced, edited and composed the music for them.

FASCINATING FACT: Adolf Hitler banned Chaplin's film *The Gold Rush*. Chaplin responded by making the film *The Great Dictator*, which made Hitler look foolish. It attacked fascists (another word for Nazis).

QUOTE: 'I was determined to go ahead, for Hitler must be laughed at.'

Start at the top of the cane at up his left arm, round the hat, down his right arm, down the right-hand leg, foot, up to his middle, other foot, up to his underarm, left side of his coat and then right.

A Recipe with International Appeal

Philip Waddell

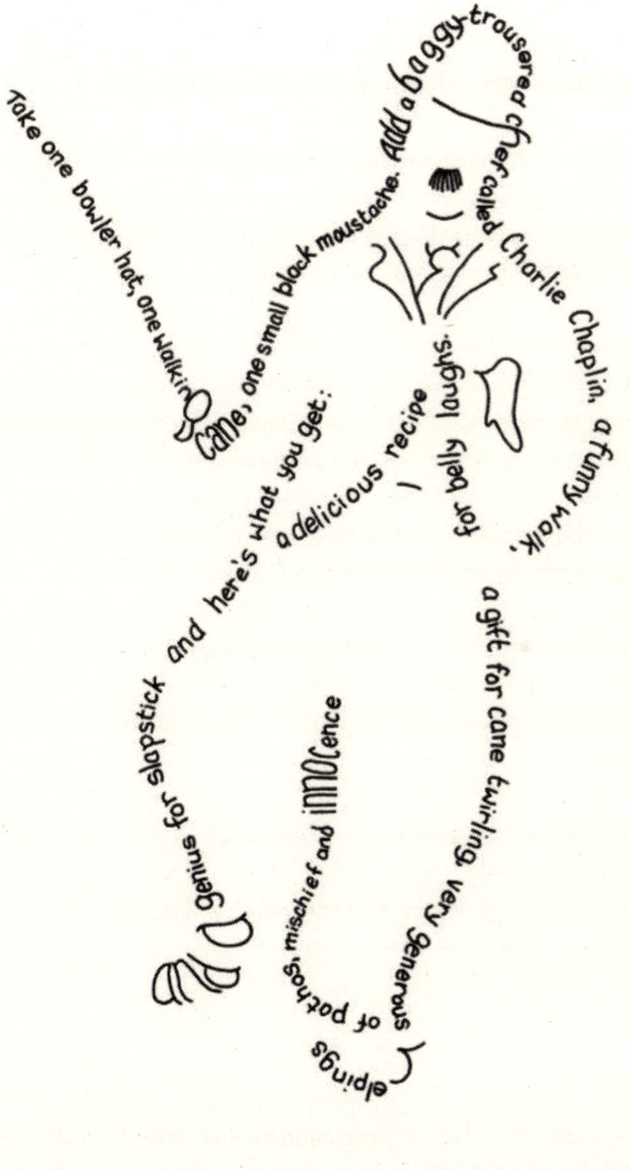
Take one bowler hat, one walking cane, one small black moustache. Add a baggy-trousered chef called Charlie Chaplin, a funny walk, a gift for cane twirling, very generous helpings of pathos, mischief and innocence and a genius for slapstick and here's what you get: a delicious recipe for belly laughs.

Georgia O'Keeffe, 1887–1986, Influenced American Modern Art

In 1985, President Ronald Reagan awarded Georgia O'Keeffe the National Medal of Arts. This is the highest honour given to artists by the United States government. She was born Georgia Totto O'Keeffe in Wisconsin, United States. She loved drawing and by the age of ten she knew she wanted to be an artist.

FAMOUS FOR: Women artists were not taken very seriously in those days and O'Keeffe was bored by her training which taught her to copy nature in her work. But after seeing paintings by the artist Arthur Wesley Dow, O'Keeffe's style gradually changed. She began to create unique abstract paintings. (Abstract means they did not try to represent the form of things exactly as they are.) People loved them and her gallery-owner husband displayed them and sold hundreds. Her most famous works were huge paintings of flowers with sweeping shapes and vivid colours.

O'Keeffe helped to begin the American modernism movement. She was also respected for her independence and as a female role model.

FASCINATING FACT: O'Keeffe enjoyed drawing humorous caricatures of her teachers while she was in school.

QUOTES: 'I found I could say things with colour and shapes that I couldn't say any other way – things I had no words for.'

'When you take a flower in your hand and really look at it, it's your world for the moment. I want to give that world to someone else.'

Start at 'you were' and read the left-hand petals down to 'painting', the outer top half-circle, the inner top half-circle, the bottom outer then inner half-circles, middle circle, then top right-hand petals 'I could' to 'hours', then down the bottom right-hand petals.

Georgia O'Keeffe

Julian Mosedale

YOU WERE
OUT THERE
ALL
ALONE
painting a path you made your own
abstract and surreal expression
your gift for nature
stuns my eye
colours dazzle lines fly by
a life of joys, of love, depression
I COULD
ENJOY YOUR WORK
FOR HOURS
BUT
MOST OF ALL
I LOVE
YOUR
FLOWERS

Emmeline Pankhurst, 1858–1928, Won UK Women the Right to Vote

In 1918, the first women in the United Kingdom were given the vote. Emmeline Goulden was born into a wealthy family, and both her parents were interested in social justice. She loved reading and one day read her mother's Women's Suffrage Journal. This was a magazine that had news about women's interests. She realised that women did not have the same opportunities as men.

FAMOUS FOR: In 1903, Pankhurst helped start the Women's Social and Political Union to get votes for women. The WSPU members were the first to be called 'suffragettes'. 'Suffrage' is an old word meaning 'vote'. After years of peaceful protest they felt that they needed to resort to deeds not words to call attention to their cause. This shocked the government and public. The government arrested suffragettes over and over again. The terrible treatment they received in jail helped get them sympathy from the public.

In 1918, an act was passed giving women the right to vote, if they were over the age of thirty and owned property. Pankhurst died a few weeks before women were granted equal voting rights with men in 1928.

FASCINATING FACT: Emmeline Pankhurst was arrested seven times before women got the vote. She has been described as one of the most influential people of the 20th Century.

QUOTE: 'The condition of our sex is so deplorable that it is our duty to break the law in order to call attention to the reasons why we do.'

Start at 'Little' and read around each petal to the end.

Emmeline Pankhurst

Sue Hardy-Dawson

Little girl in your blue jeans, do you know what freedom means? If you don't, the chances are, that you travel a well-worn path, walk in the footsteps of girls like me, who fought long for all girls' dreams. And if you don't, the chances are that you still travel a well-worn path.

Rosa Parks, 1913–2005, Helped End Racial Segregation Laws in the United States

In 1955, Rosa Parks refused to give up her seat on a bus to a white person. She was born Rosa Louise McCauley in Alabama, the United States. In the early 1900s, some states made laws which removed the rights of Black people to vote. Racial segregation (separation) was ordered in public places. Rosa watched white children being driven to school when she and her Black friends had to walk, because there were no buses for them.

FAMOUS FOR: In 1932, Rosa Parks decided to take action. She joined the National Association for the Advancement of Coloured People and became active in the civil rights movement.

Despite the civil rights movement, Parks experienced and witnessed unfair treatment and humiliation for many years. She became angry and protested on a segregated bus, refusing to move from her seat so a white person could sit down. She was arrested, found guilty at her trial and fined $10, which she refused to pay. This led to African Americans deciding to boycott the bus company for 381 days. Finally, the United States Supreme Court ended the segregation laws.

FASCINATING FACT: On the day of Rosa Parks' funeral, President George W. Bush ordered that all flags on U.S. public areas should be flown at half-mast.

QUOTE: 'I only knew that, as I was being arrested, that it was the very last time that I would ever ride in humiliation of this kind.'

Start at the top at 'because' and read left to right to the bottom.

Rosa Parks

Kate Wakeling

beca
because be
because because
because because becau
because because because beca
because because because
because she sat down to stand
up because she was fierce because because
because she burned with a fire of anger
and of love because she was as
strong and brave and true as
earth and sky and rock because she fought
for right against wrong and would
not give up no no no not for an
instant not for anything because
she was deprived of her rights and
land and because she would not that long
day be deprived of her seat because
she would not just surrender no
she would not move to the back
because she came with
hope and faith because
oh because she said 'You
must never be fearful
about what you are
doing when it is right'
because she said she came
armed only with love
because she would not give up
because she would not give up

Mahatma Gandhi, 1869–1948, Led the First Indian Civil Rights March

In 1920, Mahatma Gandhi led the first Indian civil rights movement march. Mohandas Karamchand Gandhi was born in Porbandar, Western India. He was brought up as a Hindu, believing in non-violence to all living beings. He became known as Mahatma which means 'Great Soul'. He was also affectionately called Bapu meaning father.

FAMOUS FOR: When Gandhi went to work in South Africa, he was subject to racial discrimination. On his first train trip in South Africa, even though he had a first-class ticket, he wasn't allowed to travel in first class. When he refused to move, Gandhi was thrown off the train. He led a fight against the British to secure the rights of Indians in South Africa, and also began to question the way Indians were treated in India under British rule.

On return to India he led many campaigns against the British. He showed millions of Indians how to fight against colonialism with non-violence and by civil disobedience. Civil disobedience means peacefully standing up and refusing to obey laws that you know to be wrong. In 1947, when India gained independence, Mahatma Gandhi refused positions of power in the new government, dedicating his life to the people of India.

FASCINATING FACT: Mahatma Gandhi was famous for his wire-framed, round glasses which this poem shows.

QUOTES: 'An eye for an eye will make this world blind.'

'Be the change you want to see in the world.'

Start reading the top left half-circle followed by the bottom left half-circle, then top then bottom on the right.

Gandhi's Vision

Chitra Soundar

Speak truth instead of lie,
and dare to be kind,
'cos an eye for an eye,
will make us all blind.

Nelson Mandela, 1918–2013, Fought for Black Rights in South Africa

In 1990, Nelson Mandela was released from prison. Rolihlahla Mandela was born in the small village of Mveso, South Africa. On his first day of school his teacher gave every child in the class a name in English, so he became known as Nelson.

FAMOUS FOR: Mandela grew up under the system of apartheid, which is an Afrikaans word meaning 'separation'. In South Africa, Black people were not allowed to vote, marry white people, or own property. They had to carry identification papers.

Mandela fought for his rights and those of other Black people. Because of this, he was sentenced to life in prison. After twenty-seven years, on 11 February 1990, a new South African president decided Nelson should be released. Four years later an election was held and Black South Africans were allowed to vote. After Nelson Mandela won and became South Africa's first Black president, he started uniting his country.

FASCINATING FACT: Nelson Mandela fought to get treatment for people in his country who had AIDS. His eldest son Makgatho died of this disease.

QUOTE: 'No one is born hating another person because of the colour of his skin, or his background, or his religion. People must learn to hate, and if they can learn to hate, they can be taught to love, for love comes more naturally to the human heart than its opposite.'

Start at the top half manacle at 'Born', read down to the other half of the manacle, then the chain, top line, link, bottom line, top line, bottom line, link, repeat to end, then the right-hand side of the open manacle left to right, followed by the left-hand side of the manacle.

Nelson Mandela

John Dougherty

Born into a land of black and white
he learned to see not only shades of grey,
but all the colours that would make, some day,
a rainbow of his segregated nation.
A man of peace, he saw the need to fight,
to strike a blow for those who had no voice.
Then faced the consequences of his choice,
a twenty-seven year incarceration.

Day linked to Day ten thousand times
He wrote, he thought, he learned he taught.
Meanwhile,
outside, the world changed. Walls fell; borders opened; so too
did prison gates. Released, he spoke of peace, and strove
to understand all those who had oppressed him.
Brought to power, he brought the land not
bitter justice, not
revenge or hate,
but truth and
reconciliation.

Malala Yousafzai, born 1977, Activist for Female Education

In 2012, Malala Yousafzai was shot by the Taliban. Malala Yousafzai was born in Mingora, Pakistan. Her father ran a chain of schools for girls.

FAMOUS FOR: In parts of Pakistan, the Taliban are Sunni Islam fundamentalists. They use violence to enforce women to stay at home. At times they have banned girls from school. Encouraged by her father, Yousafzai learned about political and educational issues. She started giving talks asking: 'How dare the Taliban take away my basic right to education?' Aged eleven, Yousafzai wrote a blog for BBC Urdu, about her life during the Taliban occupation of her region.

The Taliban did not like Yousafzai speaking about education and women's rights. They threatened her life. In 2012, a gunman boarded her school bus and shot her in the head in front of her friends. She received emergency treatment, and was then flown to England and operated on. Amazingly, she survived.

FASCINATING FACTS: Yousafzai has not stopped campaigning for the rights of girls to be educated and equal. She did not want revenge against the person who shot her, because she believes in peace. Aged seventeen, in 2014, she was the youngest person to receive a Nobel Peace Prize.

QUOTE: 'One child, one teacher, one book, one pen can change the world.'

Start at 'A girl' on the left outside of the head, then read the inside line of the head, then from 'Because' down the shoulder, up round the other shoulder, then the line of the book.

Malala

Michaela Morgan

A girl with a book. A girl with a book. That's what has scared them - a girl, with a book.
They get onto the bus. They call out my name. They aim. And they fire. A shot to the brain.
Because a girl with a book, a girl with a voice,
a girl with a brain, a girl with a choice, a girl with a plan to have rights,
like a man. That's what they're scared of. One girl. With a book.

ABOUT THE AUTHOR

Liz Brownlee is an award-winning poet who performs her work with her assistance dog, Lola, and also supplies Zooms or alternatives to schools, libraries, literary and nature festivals. She has fun organizing poetry retreats, exhibitions and events, and runs the poetry website Poetry Roundabout. She is a National Poetry Day Ambassador.

SHAPE SHAPERS

Truth, poem and shape by Liz Brownlee

The Socratic Method, poem Jane Clarke, shape by Liz from an idea by Jane Clarke

In a Nutshell, poem by Cheryl Moskowitz, shape by Liz from an idea by Cheryl Moskowitz

Elizabeth Blackwell, poem by Penny Kent, shape by Penny Kent and Liz

Florence Nightingale and Athena, poem and shape by Sue Hardy-Dawson

Anne Frank, poem and shape by John Dougherty

Fleming's Petri Dish, Poem and shape by Laura Mucha

Marie Curie, poem by Kate Wakeling, shape by Liz

Rosalind Franklin, poem and shape by Isabel Miles

Book of Stone, poem and shape by Mandy Coe

Jane Goodall, poem and shape by Sue Hardy-Dawson

Well on Our Way, poem by Philip Waddell, shape by Liz from an idea by Philip Waddell

The Man Who Used His Loaf, poem by Shauna Darling Robertson, shape by Liz

John Logie Baird, poem by Matt Goodfellow, shape by Liz

The Kite Experiment, poem and shape by Suzy Levinson

A Light-Bulb Moment, poem by Chrissie Gittins, shape by Liz from an idea by Chrissie Gittins

Beethoven, poem by Roger Stevens, shape by Liz from an idea by Roger Stevens

Dove Cottage Manuscript 44, poem by Gerard Benson, shape by Sue Hardy-Dawson

Albert at the Beach, poem and shape by Mark Hoadley

Expanding Forever, poem and shape by Elena de Roo

Ravi Shankar, poem by Penny Kent, shape by Penny Kent and Liz

A Bash of Inspiration, poem and shape by Kate Williams

The Wanderer, poem by Angi Lewis, shape by Liz from an idea by Angi Lewis

Chaika, poem by Myles McLeod, shape by Liz from an idea by Myles McLeod

Amelia Earhart, poem and shape by Sue Hardy-Dawson

El Draque, poem and shape by Sue Hardy-Dawson

The Climb, poem by Sam Cummings, shape by Sam Cummings and Liz

Rachel Carson, poem and shape by Liz Brownlee

Hope She Shouts, poem by Jan Dean, shape by Liz

Samuel Johnson's Dictionary of the English Language, poem by Stewart Ennis, shape by Stewart Ennis and Liz

Shakespeare, poem by Matt Goodfellow, shape by Liz

Wizard, poem by Jan Dean, shape by Liz

Sir John Tenniel, poem by Dom Conlon, shape by Dom Conlon and Liz

A Recipe With International Appeal, poem and shape by Philip Waddell

Georgia O'Keeffe, poem by Julian Mosedale, shape by Julian Mosedale and Liz

Emmeline Pankhurst, poem and shape by Sue Hardy-Dawson

Rosa Parks, poem and shape by Kate Wakeling

Gandhi's Vision, poem and shape by Chitra Soundar

Nelson Mandela, poem and shape by John Dougherty

Malala, poem by Michaela Morgan, shape by Liz